Reality Dating 101

Reality Dating 101

The Ultimate Singles' Guide for Men and Women

Kenneth Schneider

iUniverse, Inc.
New York   Bloomington   Shanghai

Reality Dating 101
The Ultimate Singles' Guide for Men and Women

Copyright © 2008 by Kenneth Schneider

All rights reserved. No part of this book may be used or reproduced by any means, graphic, electronic, or mechanical, including photocopying, recording, taping or by any information storage retrieval system without the written permission of the publisher except in the case of brief quotations embodied in critical articles and reviews.

iUniverse books may be ordered through booksellers or by contacting:

iUniverse
1663 Liberty Drive
Bloomington, IN 47403
www.iuniverse.com
1-800-Authors (1-800-288-4677)

Because of the dynamic nature of the Internet, any Web addresses or links contained in this book may have changed since publication and may no longer be valid.

The views expressed in this work are solely those of the author and do not necessarily reflect the views of the publisher, and the publisher hereby disclaims any responsibility for them.

ISBN: 978-0-595-48042-5 (pbk)
ISBN: 978-0-595-71547-3 (cloth)
ISBN: 978-0-595-60141-7 (ebk)

Printed in the United States of America

To my father, Bruce Schneider, who has stuck by me through some very difficult times. I wish everyone could experience the feeling of having a father who is on your side 100 percent of the time.

Contents

Dear Readers ... Ken's Point of View xi
Dear Readers ... Beth's Point of View xiii
Introduction xv

1 He Shoots ... He Scores? 1
   The Approach 2
   Looking in the Mirror 4

2 Computer Games 7
   Say Cheese 8
   Get a Life! 10

3 The Truth about Lies 13
   The Awkward End 14
   I've Been Cancelled Already? 16
   Is There Anything I Can Do? 18
   Playing Games 20
   I'll Call You 22
   Which Night Makes Me Important? 24

4 The Phone: Biggest Friend, Worst Enemy 27
   That First Call 28
   Voice Mails Always Work 30
   Is Talk Really Cheap? 32

I'll Talk to You Later. 34
Beep, Beep 36
Um … I Have a Life 38
Excuses, Excuses? 40
The Desperation Call. 42

5 Isn't This Supposed to Be Exciting? 45
Sports or Your Woman. 46
Late Is Not So Great 48
It's a Numbers Game 50

6 Second Helpings Are Never Better Than Firsts 53
You're Better Than Having Nothing. 54
Second Chances. 56

7 Will You Marry Me? 59
Pick This!. 60
Where's My Ring? 62
Misery or Hope 64
Why Are We Doing This? 66

8 Are You Too Ugly to Date? 69
Standing Alone 70
Do Good Looks Take Away Pain?. 72
Timing Is Everything. 74
Fix Yourself or Be Alone. 76
Accept Who You Are 78

If You Reject, You Win! 80
Ugliness Can Mean Happiness. 82
Getting Even 84
Perfume on a Pig 86
Better Looking Than I Am? 88
Does "Good Looking" Mean the Same to Everyone? 90
Looks or Intelligence 92
Can Money Buy You Love? 94
Puttin' on the Moves 96
Do Opposites Attract? 98
Which Angle Looks Best? 100
Experimenting 102

9 Random Thoughts 105
You Can't Win! 106
Whom to Believe 108
There's No Crying in Dating 110
It's Over When It's Over. 112
Do I Really Have to Bring Flowers? 114

10 Keep It Real 117
Never Quit! 118
Conclusion: The Final Talk 121

Dear Readers,

I am not a psychologist. I am simply a fifth-grade school teacher. I have not studied theories on the different brain functions of males and females. I'm just a regular guy who has been in the dating world for too long. Everything I've learned, everything I've seen, and everything I've experienced has made me come to terms with the harsh realities of dating. I'm thirty-six years old and still single. Why? Well, this book will explain why *all* single people are still single, not just myself.

    I am going to explain why meeting someone, in the dating world, can be such a difficult thing. And, unfortunately, all single people have to deal with it.

    You may disagree with what I've written, but that's only because you don't want to hear the truth. If what I've told you hits home hard, you have no other choice but to deal with it. Reality is reality, and somebody has to tell it to you the way it is.

    Each page will give you a short but true reality of single life. Many pages will hit you like a ton of bricks. But I'm not your parent, and I can tell it to you the way it is.

Kenneth Schneider

Dear Readers,

Okay, I'm not a psychologist either. I have not studied theories on the different brain functions of males and females either. I'm just a typical woman who has also been in the dating scene for a long time. I'm thirty-three years old and still looking for Mr. Right. Well, this book shows you why many women are still single, and, ladies, it's not our fault. When you hear the male perspective on things, you may be happy to still be single. I have responded to all of the male theories to show them our dating side. Kenneth Schneider, the author of this book, asked me to help him with the woman's perspective on dating. I was never so pleased to give my opinions and watch him do all the work of writing. (Of course, I had to approve of the final writing of the woman's perspective.)

As you will notice, most male realities deal with a black-and-white perspective. Most female responses go much deeper. So how do you put a black-and-white person together with a colorful person? It's hard, but it can be done.

You may disagree with some of my responses, which is okay. Women all think differently. However, I do think you'll enjoy hearing all of these "men" theories get "thrown right back at them" and make "the boys" realize that many of them are still single for a reason. So don't get frustrated upon hearing how the men think. Just enjoy how I responded for all women.

Beth

Introduction

Before the battle of the sexes begins, here are just a few things for you to remember. All of these dating realities and responses have been written by me, the author, Kenneth Schneider. I have been in many of these situations, heard about some of them from friends, and even chatted with random people about them through dating Web sites or online chat rooms as I prepared this book. Some of the ideas even came from specific people whom I have dated for mostly short periods of time. After being a part of, in some way, all of this information, I came up with the realities that you are about to read.

Beth is the person most responsible for the woman's point of view. She did not want her last name written in the book (which will hopefully change anyway when she meets the man of her realities). She has been one of the best friends I have ever had, and she always seemed to have (and still does have) opposing viewpoints about dating. We have a six-year history of friendship that dates back to when we met at a JCC playing singles' volleyball in the year 2000. We have been on the phone for countless hours discussing dating since then. And the main thing I noticed after all of our discussions about being single is that my opinions and hers have been mostly the complete opposite. Hence, the idea for the book came about.

This book was written for people who like to laugh and don't take themselves too seriously. It may sound bitter and angry at times, and goofy and ridiculous at others, but it's what makes dating what it is. So, head to your corner. Pick your side. Root for your team. And please, discuss these realities around the water cooler, on the subway, in a coffee shop, or anywhere else that a fun, heated argument can be had. Now it's time to head to class. Let's begin Reality Dating 101.

1

He Shoots ... He Scores?

Men's Dating Reality
The Approach

Have you ever seen that woman across a bar? The one you would give anything to talk to? You know, the one with the hot body and pretty face. You probably didn't have the guts to talk to her anyway, right? Well, just to make you feel better, let me tell you a secret. You wouldn't have gotten her anyway. If you are too nervous to speak to her, if you'd be sweating if she walked past you, if your heart pounds just thinking about buying her a drink, she is out of your league. Only approach women who do not make you nervous. That's the level you are on, and you may even get a date out of it.

Women's Response

A woman loves a man who seems a bit shy and nervous at first. It's kind of cute. It makes her feel more in control and makes her feel as if she has the upper hand. It doesn't mean she wouldn't date the nervous guy; it doesn't mean she wouldn't talk to him; it doesn't even mean she wouldn't accept a drink from him. It just means she will have complete control over him if they do go out. Some women really like that. And because he will be so honored to be with her, he will go along with everything she says. How much fun could that be!

Men's Dating Reality
Looking in the Mirror

If your friend has set you up on a blind date, you will learn what kind of person your friend thinks you are. If your blind date is ugly, your matchmaker thinks that you are ugly. If your blind date is pretentious, obnoxious, or a complete self-centered jerk, guess what? Your friend is showing you what he or she thinks of you.

Women's Response

If someone has set you up on a blind date, it's because that person cares about you. If the blind date doesn't go well, it's just because the two personalities didn't "click," and there was a lack of chemistry. Do not assume that your blind date's personality or level of physical attractiveness mirrors that of yours.

2
Computer Games

Men's Dating Reality

Say Cheese

Have you ever taken a photo for an online dating Web site? Did you ever look at the picture and think that you are just not photogenic, which is why the picture came out poorly? Well, let me tell you the truth. A camera is not biased toward anyone. It takes a picture of exactly what is there. If you notice, everything else in the picture looks like real life, which means so do you. If you look awful, well, that's what you look like to the rest of society. If your head looks too big, you have a big head. If you look fat, you are fat. I don't mean to hurt your feelings, but reality is reality.

Women's Response

Taking a picture is a very unrealistic way of showing what a person looks like. How many times have you seen a picture, then met the person, and noticed that this individual hardly looks like the photograph? A phony smile, a poor angle, or even use of a cheap camera can make you look worse in a picture. It's also hard to see someone's eyes and idiosyncrasies in a picture.

Men's Dating Reality

Get a Life!

A man is not supposed to send an e-mail from a dating Web site on a Friday or Saturday night to a woman. If you do, the woman receiving the e-mail will be wondering why you are home on a Friday or Saturday night. Then you will look like a loser.

Now let's think about how ridiculous that is. All of these single people who are looking to meet are afraid of being seen as losers, so they won't send an e-mail on a weekend night. But they're single. That's when they should be sending the e-mails. That's when they have the time to send them. Who feels like doing this after work?

How much respect would I gain for a guy if he wrote this e-mail to a woman he wants to date: "Hey, it's a Saturday night and I'm writing you. I'm home because I'm single. I don't want to do this during the week. I have time now. If you think I'm a loser, well, that's a stupid opinion. Oh, and by the way, can I have your number?"

Women's Response

A person is on a dating Web site to have one way of meeting people. However, sitting by a computer screen on a weekend night is not going to attract anyone. We all need to still go out with friends or be out looking for Mr. Right when we have time. The computer is there twenty-four hours a day, so why waste a weekend night staring at it? A woman would never want to know that you are looking at pictures of her on a weekend instead of socializing with the real world. That's a sign of a guy who would rather watch television on a Saturday night than take a woman out, which is the woman's worst nightmare.

3

The Truth about Lies

Men's Dating Reality
The Awkward End

At the end of a date, if the guy says, "I will call you" or "I had a great time" or "Can I see you again?" it doesn't mean anything. Those last ten seconds before a date ends are the most awkward time of the evening. A man is just being polite because he doesn't want to hurt your feelings. He would rather not have to deal with telling you that he is not interested in pursuing another date. When the phone doesn't ring the next week, you will realize he is not interested in seeing you again.

Women's Response

Any man who says, "I will call you" or "I had a great time" or "Can I see you again?" and then doesn't call is not a person you would want to date anyway. Can you imagine if a crisis occurred while you were with this person? He would probably run for the hills and leave you stranded. If he doesn't even have the guts to tell the truth to someone at the end of a date, a calamity would completely tear him apart. And when he doesn't call a few days later, a girl would realize he is not a good man and that she is better off without him.

Men's Dating Reality
I've Been Cancelled Already?

If a woman cancels on you within the first few weeks of your relationship, don't even analyze the excuse. It's a complete lie. A person would never take a chance on losing someone she really wants. And canceling is one major way of giving the signal of non-interest. So, if you're cancelled on within twenty-one days of starting a relationship, you're just not good enough for her.

Women's Response

It takes a while for a woman to become completely "into" a man. If we cancel within the first few weeks, there is usually a good reason for it. You are not a priority yet. We don't know if you are good enough for us. We just know that the beginning of a relationship is not as important to us as it is to you. You have to show us that we're important before we will not cancel. Once we feel important, then you've got us.

Men's Dating Reality
Is There Anything I Can Do?

If a woman is not interested in dating you, there is absolutely nothing you can do to change the person's mind. You look the way you do, which obviously doesn't excite that person, so being funny, acting like a gentleman, or doing the person favors will only make you feel like more of an idiot when you get rejected again and again.

Women's Response

If a person is not that into you, it can be changed. Many times, when a woman doesn't want to date someone immediately, it's because she doesn't have that "instant" attraction. However, with time, women can see less attractive men as more attractive if they have other great qualities to overcome their looks. Confidence, money, a cool job, a great car, an expensive house, or even a great bunch of friends will definitely make him look better.

Men's Dating Reality

Playing Games

If a woman is playing games with you, play games back. You are not being the bigger person by ignoring the games. Do you even want to be the bigger person? Try to make the jackass screwing with your head feel like two cents! If you can do that, you win. Then you are in control, and you will have a very happy relationship.

Women's Response

If a woman is playing games with you, it's because she's not interested in you. No intelligent woman would take a chance on losing a man that she wants by playing games. She just figures she might as well have "fun" with a less appealing man while she continues to look for the right one.

Men's Dating Reality
I'll Call You

I am so tired of hearing a woman say that she can't believe a guy didn't want to go out on a second date because he was so nice on the first date. Reality check, please! Who isn't going to be nice on a first date? I mean, you're already there. You might as well make the best of it. The rejecter is not going to say, "You know, this date really sucks. You're not what I expected. I thought you were better looking. I'm wasting my time. I'm outta here." It's just easier to be nice, go home, and never call again.

Women's Response

This is called the wimpy man syndrome. Again, as I stated earlier, any man who needs to lead a woman on during a first date, and then never calls her again, is not a real man anyway. A real man knows how to be polite, end a date as soon as possible, and let the woman know he had a good time even though she's not for him. The rare guy who can do that will eventually find Miss Right because he has the backbone for being straightforward, which is all a woman can ask for in good and bad times.

Men's Dating Reality
Which Night Makes Me Important?

If you are dating someone during the week, and never on the weekends, for more than four weeks, it's time to say goodbye. Everyone looks forward to Saturday nights more than any other night of the week. So realistically, if you are not going out on a Saturday night, you are not the thing he is looking forward to the most. Somebody else probably is.

Women's Response

If a man is not taking you out on the weekends for more than four weeks, it should be seen as an opportunity. Now you have Friday and Saturday nights to find someone better. So why not get what you can get during the week, and then dump him when a better man comes along? It's not like our wallets are getting any smaller by going out during the week.

4

*The Phone:
Biggest Friend, Worst Enemy*

Men's Dating Reality
That First Call

Talking on the phone with a potential date before meeting has absolutely no bearing on the outcome of a blind date. Some people are great phone talkers. In fact, it is so much easier to talk to someone on a phone because you are not being judged by the way you look. Your true personality can come out. But unfortunately, a blind date is not about personality. It's about the first two seconds and if the other person is attracted to you. And even worse, the better you are on the phone, the higher the expectation is for you when you arrive on the date, which will make you feel horrible if you get rejected. That shows you how important good looks really are, and you must come to the conclusion that you just don't have them.

Women's Response

The phone conversation before a blind date is extremely important. You will not even get to a first date if that chat is poor. Do you know how scary it is for a woman to sit across the table from a man and have nothing to say? The more interesting a man is, the more attractive a woman will see him. So, yes, it's true the first few seconds of a blind date are important, but they're not make-or-break. A man's looks go up tremendously if he is well-spoken.

Men's Dating Reality
Voice Mails Always Work

If you leave a message on voice mail or a machine, and you don't get a call back, don't try again. You were rejected by her. She did get the message. Everyone gets their messages. Nothing was wrong with her answering machine or voice mail. What do you have to lose by calling her again? More self-esteem. Move on and lower your expectations.

Women's Response

If you leave a message on her voice mail or machine, and you don't get a call back, you were not necessarily rejected. Sometimes we have so many messages on our voice mails that we take our time listening to them and then make a list of all the people we have to call back. And you all know how women can talk. Our conversations can go on for hours, so we may not have time to call back immediately. Also, when we first meet someone, it does not mean as much to us as it does to guys, so calling again can't hurt. Many women like aggressive men who will call a few times to show they're really interested.

Men's Dating Reality
Is Talk Really Cheap?

Analyzing your relationship on the phone with a friend is pathetic. It's not going to change what was said. It's not going to change what was done. "Why did she do this?" "Why did she say that?" "What does this mean?" "What does that mean?" Come on, how the hell is your buddy supposed to know? He wasn't there. So do your friends a favor, shut up, and go do something productive.

Women's Response

Analyzing your relationship with a friend is a great way to vent and try to understand your partner better. It's always good to hear another perspective from a person who is not in that situation. When someone who is on the outside looking in is trying to help you, it's much clearer to that person because emotions aren't involved. It's always hard to think clearly when you are directly involved in an important circumstance.

Men's Dating Reality
I'll Talk to You Later

If you are on the phone with a potential date on a Monday or Tuesday, and you're told he'll know by Thursday if he's free for the weekend, don't even think about analyzing this one. He is trying to do better than you. He has more calls to make, or he is waiting for callbacks. If he can't find someone more attractive than you, you'll get the nod for that weekend. But the same deal will occur the next weekend. If you go out with him, you deserve to be treated terribly.

Women's Response

Wow! We actually have something to agree upon. If a man can't give you a solid answer for the weekend by Monday or Tuesday, he is most likely not the one for you. However, when you get the Thursday call, if your weekend is still available, you might as well see him. Again, you will get a free meal, and you will be taken to a movie that you don't have to pay for. If it happens again the next week, keep doing the same thing. And when you do meet a better person, you can tell the first guy where to go over the weekend!

Men's Dating Reality
Beep, Beep

If you are on the phone having a conversation with a potential date, and he gets that dreaded beep (call waiting), and he tells you he needs to take the call, here's what just happened. Someone more attractive than you called him, and that person is more important than you. No guy would ever answer a call waiting if he is about to "land" the woman of his dreams. The person beeping in is the person he is excited about, and he doesn't care if he's being rude to you. Why should he be, you've now dropped down to at least second. If you choose to pick up the phone and still go out with him, if and when he calls you back, you are a loser. You should be ashamed of yourself and your low self-esteem.

Women's Response

If a man needs to take another call when you are talking to him, who gives a damn? This gives us time to call our girlfriends back, or even call back another potential date. Women are not so needy that we worry about who you are talking to. We will assume the truth until we find out otherwise.

Men's Dating Reality
Um … I Have a Life

If a woman tells you she couldn't call you because she is too busy, she's lying. I have never met a person who couldn't take the time to dial seven or ten digits to say hello in a twenty-four-hour day, unless this person was unmotivated to call you. If you have enough time to use the restroom four times a day, you could easily find the time to call someone once.

Women's Response

Believe it or not, guys, women do have lives. We are not at your beck and call like it was in the fifties. There are times when we actually can't call you because of problems with friends, family, or even work. Don't be so egotistical and think you have to always be on our "calling list" for that day. What's the big deal if you wait one more day? Maybe tomorrow night, we'll be able to relax, sit on the couch, and have a great conversation.

Men's Dating Reality
Excuses, Excuses?

If you call a potential date's or your girlfriend's cell phone and you get her voice mail, it is because she saw that you were the one calling. She does not want to talk. Don't even believe the "I was driving" excuse or "I didn't hear it ring." That's a load of garbage. People cling to their cell phones all day long. So, yes, your call was not picked up because she didn't feel like speaking with the person dialing the digits.

Women's Response

If a man is that insecure to think that his woman or a potential date would not want to talk to him, than you are in for a rough relationship. Believe it or not, women may actually be driving when the phone rings and don't want to get a ticket or into an accident when talking on the phone. Sometimes cell phones don't even ring. Don't worry, boys. If the woman is "into you," she will call you back. Just leave a message after the sound of the tone.

Men's Dating Reality
The Desperation Call

If you have been out with a guy one to three times, and then you do not hear from him again until one week or longer, don't even think about seeing him again. It's called the desperation call. The caller had a number of dates lined up over the past few weeks. You were not at the top of the list; however, all of the other dates fell through. So you are the back-up plan. If you choose to see him again, I will guarantee the same thing will happen to you once this person finds someone better than you. The only thing worse than the man making the desperation call is the extremely desperate woman who agrees to go out again.

Women's Response

If you have been out with a guy one to three times, and then you do not hear from him again until one week or longer, you should see him again if you have nothing better going on. Except this time, have fun with him. Order the most expensive dinner on the menu. Order dessert. Tell him you want to see a play, not a movie. Don't act uninterested. Act more interested. If he is that desperate to call you again, make him pay.

5

Isn't This Supposed to Be Exciting?

Men's Dating Reality
Sports or Your Woman

If you are dating a man who chooses to play or watch a sporting event over spending time with you, it is because he thinks the event is more exciting than you. No one ever chooses to do the thing that's less exciting. Would a guy rather walk around a mall or watch a football game? Would a guy rather go to a musical or look at cars? I think the answers are obvious. Human beings naturally head toward the more exciting thing.

Women's Response

If you are dating a man who chooses to play or watch a sporting event over spending time with you, you need to get even with him by adding hobbies to your life at the times when he needs you the most. You know those moments when he is feeling badly about work, or the times that his family is having a party for a distant cousin? You don't have time for that. Your favorite show is on TV, or your girlfriend is having a crisis and you just must go. That will teach him.

Men's Dating Reality
Late Is Not So Great

If your boyfriend is consistently late, it's because he is not that excited about you. What man is ever late for something he's excited about? If the movie starts at 9:00, he's there by 9:00. If the football game starts at 1:00, he's sitting in front of the TV (with food) by 1:00. If Friday night poker begins at 8:00, he's dealing the cards by 8:00. So if he's not there by 7:30 for your Saturday night date, well guess what? It's because he's not excited about you!

Women's Response

If your man is consistently late and it really bothers you, don't complain about it. That will just give him more power over you. Here's what you should do. When he finally arrives for the date, make sure you talk on your cell phone in the car to annoy him. Or focus on filing your nails while he is driving. And lastly, constantly look in the mirror while he is trying to talk to you and keep fixing your make-up. This way he can't spend quality time with you when he wants to.

Men's Dating Reality
It's a Numbers Game

If you are very excited about the woman you are with, she is not that excited about you. If you are not excited about her, she will adore you. Here's why. We all strive to be the best we can be. (At least, we should be doing that.) So we strive to get the best-looking woman we possibly can. This means we are looking at women to date who are better looking than we are. Unfortunately, they're doing the same thing. So, if you're a six in looks on a scale of one to ten, you are striving to get a seven. Well, that seven is striving to get an eight. And the eight wants a nine, and so on. The reality is that until we all finally realize that dating our own number is the only way to be successful, we will all keep reaching for the stars and coming down with just the gas.

Women's Response

If you are a player, you are 100 percent correct. But most of us are not players. We are just looking for the rare decent man who will adore us and treat us the way we deserve to be treated. It's not about numbers. It's not about who is better than whom. Men try to make this into a black-and-white game. Remember, women look at the whole package a man can bring. We don't number you guys on a scale of one to ten. It's pretty scary to think that guys do that to us and that they think we do the same to them. It's just not the way women were created.

6

Second Helpings Are Never Better Than Firsts

Men's Dating Reality
You're Better Than Having Nothing

If a man dumps you and then comes back into your life to try it again, guess what? He doesn't love you more. He didn't make a mistake. He didn't all of a sudden figure things out. He realized that he's not as attractive as he thought he was, and you're good enough for him right now. Nobody else that he's attracted to wants to date him. It's a horrible conclusion for a man to come to, but it happens. He has to decide if he would rather be alone the rest of his life or be with a woman who is desperate enough to have a loveless relationship with him.

Women's Response

If a woman allows a man back into her life after getting dumped, she is actually using him as a safety net until the next man comes along. She knows she was a rebound, but so is he. So why not make the best of it for the time being and get some free meals. The sad part is when the male thinks he's outsmarting the female. We know exactly what he's trying to do. But again, if you're still single, why not let him back in. And then eventually, when a new man comes along, you can stab the first guy in the back.

Men's Dating Reality
Second Chances

Never give a woman a second chance if she dumped you the first time you went out. It's the same person. Do you think she has really changed? Do you think all of a sudden you will be treated well? As they say, "A leopard never changes her spots." So what do you think is going to change this time around? Nothing! Maybe things will be different for the first few weeks. But watch how things quickly revert back to the way they were. Just raise your self-esteem and move on.

Women's Response

How many people have broken up, gotten back together, and eventually married? I bet if you asked a hundred couples, at least 10 percent of them would be in that category. People think differently at different stages of their lives, and this includes their thoughts about relationships. Just because a woman wasn't ready to be with you one year, it doesn't mean that she wouldn't be ready for a relationship with you in the future.

7
Will You Marry Me?

Men's Dating Reality
Pick This!

If all of your friends are getting married and you're the only one left who is not, it doesn't mean you're more picky than they. It means that no one is interested in you. Honestly, I'm tired of hearing people in their thirties say, "I'm just pickier than most." Or "I don't want to settle." Well, the facts are the facts. Most people are single in their twenties, so all of the good people are still available. Of course, those people are going to be taken in their twenties. Who wouldn't want to date a good person? If you are still single in your thirties, the sad truth is that you have made so many mistakes in your dating life, and you are just trying to cover up for them by saying, "Now I know what I'm looking for." Well, why did all of your friends know what they were looking for when they were in their twenties, except for you?

Women's Response

If all of your friends are getting married and you're the only one left who is not, it means that you have not met Mr. Right yet. Why would you settle for someone you're not excited about? Then if you choose to settle, you'd be in for a whole new set of problems. People are staying single longer these days. Many people want to get their careers started. Some women dated horrible men for too long in their twenties because they were too naive. Some women are even so independent that a man is a bonus, not a need. And don't forget, if you settle and marry too soon, you can't date the person you've always wanted to. If you hold out and not follow the crowd, you may just be the smart one and get exactly what you want.

Men's Dating Reality
Where's My Ring?

If you have been dating the same man for more than five years without an engagement, you are a complete sucker. Even if a proposal happens, it's not because of love, it's because of laziness. Who wouldn't want to secure someone great for a lifetime? Who would take a chance on losing a great woman? So, if it's been five years or more, the man has realized that it would be easier to stay with you than to try and find someone else. Dump him quickly or live a loveless marriage.

Women's Response

If you have been dating the same man for more than two years without an engagement, it's time to ask questions. Who would be with someone for five years and still not know where her future lies? Five years is an eternity, and a big waste of time. When you ask him questions, if you don't like the answers, run away as fast as you can.

Men's Dating Reality
Misery or Hope

Single people *hate* engaged people. The single person may say he is happy for you, but it's not true. The single person is so jealous of the engaged person because he cannot find what the engaged person has found. The worst feeling is when a lonely, single person picks up the phone and hears, "Guess what? I just got engaged." That's like a poor person hearing that his friend (who was also poor) won the lottery. Now, who's he going to bitch to about being poor?

Women's Response

Finding out that a girlfriend got engaged is one of the best things a woman could hear. It shows that there is hope. Love actually exists, and if it happened to a friend who is close to you, it will eventually happen to you also. From another perspective, when a friend gets engaged, that's one fewer woman on the market. It takes away a little competition for you.

Men's Dating Reality
Why Are We Doing This?

Dating is not a lot of fun. I mean, think about it. We all strive to find that perfect match. We date and we date and we date. I reject you, you reject me, blah, blah, blah. Then finally, we find our "perfect" match. This is the person we will marry. So finally, the wedding occurs. Then the odds tell us that we will get divorced. So you fight and fight and fight to reach this goal, and the marriage will probably fail anyway. We're all crazy. Guys, watch sports and gamble! Women, hang out with your girlfriends and shop! Wouldn't life be a lot simpler for all of us?

Women's Response

Dating is a lot of fun. How many times in your life do you get to meet so many different people? Where else can you come up with so many fascinating stories to tell your friends (good or bad)? Where else can you get free meals, free movie tickets, go to free concerts, or even have a chance to meet the man of your dreams? It does happen if you relax and enjoy the ride. And if you stay patient, and wait for the right one, a divorce will not occur. If you rush into something, it never works anyway.

8

Are You Too Ugly to Date?

Men's Dating Reality
Standing Alone

If you go to a club or a bar and a man doesn't approach you, it's because you're ugly. Stop making excuses for yourself. You are who you are. Have you ever seen an attractive woman standing by herself? It never happens.

Women's Response

If you go to a club or a bar and a man doesn't approach you, it's because he's intimidated by you. He is afraid of rejection. Many men need higher self-esteem. All those guys standing by the wall drinking a beer would love to approach you. But obviously, the wall won't reject them.

Men's Dating Reality
Do Good Looks Take Away Pain?

If a woman tells you that she can't date you because she is trying to get over someone else, it's a load of crap. You're just not attractive enough for her. Any person can get over someone else when an appealing looking person approaches. If you're not a good-looking man, why would she want to get over her last boyfriend for you?

Women's Response

If a woman tells you that she can't date you because she is trying to get over someone else, it has nothing to do with attraction. It actually could be the truth. Many times, women don't want to rush back into a relationship as quickly as men. We need to get to know a person, and unfortunately, that takes time. We don't just see a handsome face and say, "Yes, I'm ready." Women look for the whole package.

Men's Dating Reality
Timing Is Everything

If you go on a blind date to a coffee shop, or a bar, and the woman you are meeting ends the date in one hour or less, you are ugly. If you weren't, she wouldn't have left so quickly. Think about it. If you are attracted to someone, do you ever want to leave? So please, guys, save your self-esteem and don't give her another call. It's just going to make you feel uglier than you already are.

Women's Response

If you go on a blind date to a coffee shop, and the woman you are meeting ends the date in one hour or less, it's not only about your looks. It could also be your breath, your conceitedness, your vanity, or how much you talk about your ex. And don't forget, we may have set up a number of dates for that day. So, if the date does end in less than an hour, it could just be because of timing and not about you. Why not call again? It would show the woman you are assertive, and we like that.

Men's Dating Reality
Fix Yourself or Be Alone

The main reason a woman rejects you, or breaks up with you, is because she doesn't think you're attractive enough for her. There are so many guys who are bigger than you and better looking than you. Maybe it's time you went to the gym or looked closely at your face to see what you could do to improve yourself. Do you have a big nose? Get a nose job. Are you going bald? Get a hair transplant. Stop analyzing why your relationship ended. Either try to fix yourself or just deal with not being attractive enough for certain types of women.

Women's Response

There are many reasons why a woman would reject you other than your looks. You can be cheap, lazy, unmotivated, spend too much time with your friends, gamble, or watch too much sports. How is getting a nose job or a hair transplant going to change a cheap, lazy, unmotivated person? How will that stop him from gambling and watching sports? It won't. So if you're going to fix yourself, you're probably going to need to do more than just fix your face.

Men's Dating Reality
Accept Who You Are

If you get rejected sometimes, and accepted other times, guess what? You're an average-looking man, and you will only be able to date an average-looking woman. Uglier women will like you. Good-looking women won't. Get used to it. As the "professionals" say, "Accept yourself for who you are." Stop dreaming of reaching for the stars, it ain't happening. Reality is reality. And you'll be much happier once you accept that. So stop trying for the hotties. You'll never get them. Date someone on your level and live an average life.

Women's Response

If a guy gets rejected sometimes, and accepted other times, guess what? You just may have more in common with some women than others. Even the hotties will date a less attractive man if she feels she will get along with him. If he is confident in himself and doesn't show insecurities about the way he looks, he has an even better chance. I have seen very attractive women with average-looking men many times. All of these men have one thing in common (and no, it's not always money). It's a belief in who they are. Women don't like to walk all over men. We only do it when we lack respect for you.

Men's Dating Reality
If You Reject, You Win!

People say that it doesn't matter who rejected whom. Hell, it doesn't. At least if you do the rejecting, you're not as ugly as the other person. Now this may seem a bit harsh, but how awful does it feel to be rejected on a first date. You know it's because of your looks. So if you can get out of the date showing no interest, you will not have to deal with any loss of self-esteem. The other person will.

Women's Response

It really doesn't matter who rejects whom. The bottom line is that it's over because there wasn't enough chemistry and communication. To base your self-esteem on the way a person looks at you physically is disgusting. Only a man would say that. Dating is not about getting possessions for your ego. It's about meeting a person you connect with mentally and physically.

Men's Dating Reality
Ugliness Can Mean Happiness

If an ugly man can just accept that he's ugly and date an ugly woman, it will make the best marriage. Think about it. It would be two people who couldn't cheat on each other, even if they wanted to. Unless, of course, one of them decided to cheat with another ugly person, and what's the point of that? You might as well stay with the person you are comfortable with and play games all night. I wouldn't recommend Twister, but Scrabble and Monopoly are fun! So this couple will have to accept each other, which good-looking couples have trouble doing because of temptation, and be in bliss through eternity.

Women's Response

There is no such thing as an ugly woman. If a man would just stop and see what's on the inside of a girl once in a while, he may end up happier than he ever thought he could be. Every woman is beautiful in her own way. Some of us may not have that outward appeal but are sweet as sugar on the inside. Some of us are giving to a fault. Some of us, yes, guys, it's true, are extremely smart. And wouldn't it be nice to have a great conversation now and then. So if an ugly *man thinks he's getting an ugly wife, he should stay single forever and save his money for a big, fat dog.*

Men's Dating Reality
Getting Even

If a woman rejects you, you can't get even with her. So don't even give it a shot. The more you try, the more desperate you look. It's just like sending the same resume to a company that already has said no to you five times. If the resume hasn't changed, why would you be wanted by the business now? Just move on and realize that if you were better looking, you wouldn't have been rejected in the first place.

Women's Response

If a woman tells you that she doesn't want to date you, you can get even with her. I shouldn't be telling the men this, but here it goes. Just keep calling her, sending her e-mails, and writing her letters. It will freak her out to no end. But, guys, this will never work in getting her to like you. C'mon, be smarter than that! We like assertive, not crazy.

Men's Dating Reality
Perfume on a Pig

It doesn't matter where you buy your clothes or how much you spend on them. A good-looking man will look good in anything, and an ugly guy will look terrible in everything. Have you ever heard of the saying, "You can't put perfume on a pig?" So if you're ugly, don't worry about wasting money on your clothes, just deal with who you are.

Women's Response

Clothes make the man. In fact, the clothes a guy wears, and how he wears them, will give you a good idea about the person himself. A neatly dressed guy is usually an organized person. A man who wears clothes from five years ago is usually not too wealthy. A man who doesn't match his colors is probably going to be a very disorganized person. And, finally, if a guy shows up on a date in a T-shirt and ripped jeans, do I need to say anymore? He is not getting a second date whether he is or isn't ugly. How embarrassing would it be to be seen in public with him dressed like a bum?

Men's Dating Reality
Better Looking Than I Am?

No matter how good looking you are, or you think you are, there is always someone better looking than you. Believe it or not, that's a good thing. It means your self-esteem shouldn't take a complete plunge if and when you get dumped. I mean, if there are better-looking people than you, getting dumped is bound to happen. On the other hand, you will most likely find someone else to date because, obviously, other people have been dumped before as well. Even gorgeous Hollywood actors go through break-ups, so it can definitely happen to you.

Women's Response

Okay, this is why women get so pissed off at men. They can't even see this, but dating is not about looks alone. If Hollywood actors get dumped, it obviously goes deeper than just the surface. Believe it or not, personality matters too. And, yes, if you break up, you will find someone else. What makes it difficult to stay in a relationship is that it's hard to find someone whose personality "clicks" with yours so you are attracted to him. That's why the search for some of us seems to be endless.

Men's Dating Reality

Does "Good Looking" Mean the Same to Everyone?

Beauty is not in the eye of the beholder. If it were, why would most men chase after the same women and ignore the rest? Try this game. Show a group of men three pictures of three different women. And I'll bet you at least 90 percent of the group thinks the same woman is the best looking. At least 90 percent will agree on the worst looking, and obviously the same percentage will agree on woman number two.

Women's Response

Trust me, beauty is in the eye of the beholder, at least for women. I have seen more outwardly attractive women with less attractive men than the opposite. It's because women can get past the layers and see what a man is really like on the inside. How? We ask questions, we notice confidence, and we want to be with a respectful person. Men chase the same women all of the time because beauty is "skin deep" to most of them. That's why many of you get treated like trash.

Men's Dating Reality
Looks or Intelligence

Good-looking people have better lives than ugly people. They have more people to talk to because the average person likes to look at an attractive face. They can select who they want to date because people love to be seen with a good-looking partner. They are respected more by society because people think good looks means intelligence and confidence. Is it fair? No! Is it reality? Yes!

Women's Response

Actually, intelligent people have much better lives than unintelligent people regardless of how they look. If you can solve problems, put things in perspective, and understand why things happen, you are better able to deal with life, whether you are outwardly beautiful or not. Good looks are short lived. In comparison, intelligence lasts a lifetime. What girl would want to be seen with a handsome face if the man can't help with the bills, fix a broken door, or write her a love note? Only intelligent people can do those things or at least learn how.

Men's Dating Reality

Can Money Buy You Love?

Dating is expensive for men. But the reality is this: It doesn't have to be. No need to impress the ladies. No need to go out of your way. If a woman is into you, you can take her on a cheap date, and she'll appreciate it. If you are ugly, you can eat at a four-star restaurant in mid-town Manhattan and go to a Broadway show and still get blown off in the same night.

Women's Response

Dating is expensive for men because women are worth it. You're not buying a toy here; you're trying to impress us so we'll want to be with you. Trust me, no one will want to date you if you think watching television is a weekly Saturday night event no matter how attractive you are. No, we don't need the most expensive stuff to be impressed with you; however, going out of your way will help your cause to no end.

Men's Dating Reality
Puttin' on the Moves

If you are with a man who doesn't "put the moves" on you, it's because you are not attractive. When a man finds a woman appealing, trust me on this, he can't keep his hands off her. Guys don't have intimacy issues. We have attraction issues. So, he is with you because he thinks you are the best he can do, and he is trying to figure out if he can deal with that for the rest of his life.

Women's Response

If you are with a man who doesn't "put the moves" on you, he is actually showing respect for who you are. Not every man needs to have his ego built by getting down a woman's pants. Some men actually want to wait for the right moment or until the woman shows that she is ready. It would be pretty sad for a man to be with a woman if he wasn't attracted to her. Why wouldn't he just get a dog or a blow-up doll? When a man treats your body with respect, that is when you know you've met Mr. Right.

Men's Dating Reality
Do Opposites Attract?

Opposites do not attract. How often do you see an ugly person with an attractive person? How often do you see a brain surgeon with a blue-collar worker? How often do you see a fat woman with a skinny man? Think about it.

Women's Response

Opposites do not attract? How do older men wind up with younger women? Why are women willing to date overweight men if they have great personalities? Why do nice, intelligent women date construction workers? It's definitely not for their brains.

Men's Dating Reality
Which Angle Looks Best?

This is going to sound ridiculous, but it's true. I call it the dating angle. Yes, the dating angle. Have you ever dated a woman who looks good at certain angles, but not others? I mean, she looks good with her head turned to the left, but she looks weird with her head turned to the right. Or she looks good close up but not far away. I bet it's happened to all of you. This date is really confusing. What are you supposed to do? Be excited on certain days when you see only the angles you like to see? Or be excited for two of the four hours of the date? Eventually, you'll have to make a decision if a partly good-looking person, and a partly weird-looking person, is for you.

Women's Response

Again, if being attracted to someone is only "skin deep," then the angle at which a person stands must be really important. When a woman doesn't "look as good," say, turned to the left, as she does, say, straightforward, is she still an interesting person to talk to? Is she still intelligent? Well, if she is, she'll figure out your "angle," and she will run away from you as fast as she can 100 percent of the time.

Men's Dating Reality Experimenting

In the dating world, hot-looking people are mean. Ugly people are nice. Average-looking people are, well, average. They don't know how to act. They act nicely to the hot people and act mean to the ugly people. Try this experiment if you can. Take a really hot girl. Bring on an even hotter guy, and watch how nice she becomes. Or take a really ugly girl. Bring on an even uglier guy, and watch how poorly she treats him. People don't have the patience for talking to people below their level. Yet they have all the patience in the world for talking to people above their level. That's just the way it is.

Women's Response

Why don't you try this experiment? Show a hot woman a confident, less attractive man who has a good head on his shoulders with an appealing job, and you will see her talk to him for hours. The problem is that most less attractive men lack confidence in themselves, so the hotties won't speak to them. Who wants to be with a person who lacks confidence? Also, show me a hot girl who will give the time of day to a hot guy if he is self centered, lacking self-esteem about his job, or more into looking in the mirror than at her. It just won't happen.

9
Random Thoughts

Men's Dating Reality

You Can't Win!

If you are single, not only are you lonely, but you have to pay higher taxes.

Women's Response

What the hell are you talking about? A typical male brain making no sense at all! Honestly, women always have women friends to hang out with. So don't think that if a woman doesn't have a man, she's lonely. A man is a bonus, not a need. Wow, and we're trying to meet the right one of these people?

Men's Dating Reality

Whom to Believe

Never believe what your friends and family tell you about your dating life. Reality check here. They are your friends and family for a reason. They are going to tell you what you want to hear, if they care about you. Believe the people who have nothing to lose when they insult you. These people see you for who you really are. For example, if your friend says your haircut looks good, and a coworker says it doesn't look good, believe the coworker. The coworker is speaking based on an immediate reaction; your family is speaking based on what your reaction will be. If your family says you will meet a great woman to marry one day, and a person at the gym says you won't, then you won't. Sorry! It's nice to be encouraged, but all of our parents think we should wind up with a caring, sweet, beautiful person. But c'mon now, how many people actually get that type of a person?

Women's Response

Your family and friends have your best interest at heart. They want to see you happy. Isn't that why they are close with you? They don't want to see you get hurt, so they will tell you the truth. Believing someone you hardly know makes absolutely no sense. That person could be bitter or have had a bad day. How many times do people make jokes at someone else's expense just for a rise out of others in the area? Who would believe a stranger or an acquaintance over a relative or friend? That's ridiculous.

Men's Dating Reality
There's No Crying in Dating

If a man cries to show his sensitive side, it's not that he's sensitive, he's a weak man. A man shouldn't cry. If he does, he should be dumped fast. If a guy cries at sensitive moments, think about what he will do during times of crises. Would you want to be with a man who pulls out a Kleenex during a car accident? Would it make you feel good to see this guy shed tears if there was a flood in the house? Who respects a crier?

Women's Response

Women love men who can cry. What is better than a sensitive man? Women don't bottle up their feelings, so why would we want men to? A guy can be big, tough, and strong, and still cry. The caveman days are over. Keeping everything inside can ruin a relationship, not help it. If something hurts, why not let it out? A man in touch with his emotions would make for the best father and a loving husband.

Men's Dating Reality
It's Over When It's Over

If you and/or your girlfriend are seeking counseling about your relationship, the relationship is over. There are too many people out there to meet to be wasting your time with counseling. The dating scene is an intimidating place, but seeing a counselor is not going to make your partner become Miss or Mr. America. And we're all stuck with our personalities. Take it or leave it. A social worker can't change that. Seeing a counselor is the same thing as saying, "I'm just too damn lazy to look for someone new, so I'll pay a counselor to help me figure out a way to keep me in this hell a little bit longer." Or by seeing a counselor, you're saying, "I don't think I can find anyone else, so I better make this work."

Women's Response

Going to counseling actually makes you a better, stronger person. You can learn more about yourself and your partner, which will help you better express your feelings with the person you are dating. It's not about changing your looks or personality. It's about seeing things with a new perspective. When you care about someone, you'll try to change. You just can't keep moving on to new partners every time something isn't as you like it. Giving up on a relationship makes you a quitter, and no woman would ever want that.

Men's Dating Reality
Do I Really Have to Bring Flowers?

If a man never brings flowers, candy, or any surprise gifts on a date, it's because he feels he can get away without doing it. Think about it. For her birthday, she gets a gift. For Valentine's Day, she gets a gift. For Christmas, she gets a gift. Why? Because a guy cannot get away without bringing one. He will hear about it forever. So if a lady is receiving absolutely nothing on a regular basis, it's because the man is comfortable. The woman who gets gifts on a regular basis simply keeps the man on edge all of the time, so she can get what she wants.

Women's Response

This is where men have it all backwards. If you want to have your way with a woman, listen to this. We don't judge you on birthday gifts, Christmas gifts, and Valentine's gifts. We judge you on the surprise gifts. That shows you care. So if you think you are getting away without getting us presents on "regular days," just think about how many fewer times we will cook for you, call you back quickly, or watch you play sports.

10
Keep It Real

Men's Dating Reality
Never Quit!

The people who say that you will meet a woman when you least expect it, not when you are looking for someone, are as blind as two people wish they were on a bad blind date. How many times has a terrific woman seen you at the supermarket and asked you out? How many times have you been walking down the street when Ms. Wonderful has approached? Yes, it's not great to be so obsessed with looking that you lose your focus on other areas of life that interest you. However, if you are not looking, you will not find. If you are looking, you have a chance. It may be frustrating, ego bruising, and pure hell to be out there with yourself constantly on the line. But it's still better than the alternative. And I don't think they sell too many books on how to be a quitter.

Women's Response

How many great relationships have happened when you least expected it? Did you ever go to a friend's party and a great guy was there? How about that new man at work? Meeting someone playing in a coed sporting league happens all the time. The key is to just enjoy your life. When you do, you will be exposed to more people. You never know when one of them will approach you and ask you out. You also never know when someone has a brother to set you up with. The key is exposure. The more exposure you have to people, the better your chances of meeting someone. But I do agree with one thing from the male perspective. Quitting is not an option. If you truly want to meet someone, you absolutely will.

Conclusion: The Final Talk

From the time two people meet each other, to the time they will never see each other again, there is always so much uncertainty. Will he call again? Will she pick up the phone? Does he still like me? Am I the only one she is seeing? Can I trust him? Do I picture a future with her? It goes on and on and on. The questions never end, and the answers are few and far between. You just never know when that final conversation will happen.

People like to be in control of their lives, and with dating, people lose this control, and it drives us crazy. Most of us were taught that if you strive hard enough for something, you will get it. Well, in dating, it is only 50 percent in your hands. The other 50 percent is primarily luck.

This book was not intended to discourage you from reaching your dreams. In fact, it's a book that could help you if you stay within its terms of reality. Striving for the "best you can get" is great. But be real about it. You are who you are. So start dating people who match you. It may not be that "hot blonde" whom you would give your left arm to speak with. But it can still be a quality person. Just carefully look at yourself in the mirror and think about who would like you. Once you realize that, enjoy who you can get, instead of being discouraged by who you can't.

So, the final talk is about over. You've been warned this time. And who knows, maybe in a short while, we can all graduate to Reality Dating 102!

978-0-595-48042-5
0-595-48042-X

Lightning Source UK Ltd.
Milton Keynes UK
02 October 2009

144444UK00001B/234/P